PRAISE FOR GABRIEL FI[TZMAURICE]

"[T]he best contemporary, traditional, p[oet]"
Ray Olson, BOOKLIS[T]

"Fitzmaurice is a wonderful poet".
Giles Foden, THE GUARDIAN

"One of Ireland's favourite poets".
BOOKS IRELAND

"Gabriel Fitzmaurice's...ballads...are comparable with Burns's for their insights and lyricism".
James J.McAuley, THE IRISH TIMES

"Fitzmaurice's elevation of Moyvane has resonances with Oliver Goldsmith's Auburn and Patrick Kavanagh's Shancoduff".
Brendan Hamill, FORTNIGHT

"Ireland, particularly the South...finds its local bard in Gabriel Fitzmaurice...thereby making such 'singing' socially responsible in a way Wordsworth would have endorsed".
Francis O'Hare, THE HONEST ULSTERMAN

"[Fitzmaurice] is poetry's answer to John B. Keane".
Fred Johnston, BOOKS IRELAND

"We need poets who can probe reality like this, and Fitzmaurice is doing it in style".
Gerard Quinn, THE KERRYMAN

"He has a gift for making the quotidian interesting and investing the ordinary with extraordinary significance".
Gearóid Mac Lochlainn, THE CELTIC PEN

"Gabriel Fitzmaurice finds truths that speak to us all".
Moyra Donaldson, FIGMENTS (Belfast)

Poems of Faith and Doubt

Poems of Faith and Doubt

GABRIEL FITZMAURICE

with bog paintings by
BRENDA FITZMAURICE

salmonpoetry

For Les Murray

Published in 2011 by
Salmon Poetry
Cliffs of Moher, County Clare, Ireland
Website: www.salmonpoetry.com
Email: info@salmonpoetry.com

Copyright © Gabriel Fitzmaurice, 2011

ISBN 978-1-907056-69-7

All rights reserved. No part of this publication may be reproduced or transmitted in any form or by any means, electronic or mechanical, including photography, recording, or any information storage or retrieval system, without permission in writing from the publisher. The book is sold subject to the condition that it shall not, by way of trade or otherwise, be lent, resold or otherwise circulated without the publisher's prior consent in any form of binding or cover other than that in which it is published and without a similar condition, including this condition, being imposed on the subsequent purchaser.

ARTWORK: Brenda Fitzmaurice
COVER DESIGN: Siobhán Hutson

Salmon Poetry receives financial support from The Arts Council

Acknowledgements

Acknowledgements are due to the following where these poems first appeared:

Quadrant (Australia): 'Ruckard Drury', 'A Product to Sell', 'The Traveller Woman', 'To my Son as he Leaves Home', 'To my Daughter, Pregnant', 'A Happy Marriage', 'Death of a Playwright', 'Death of a Poet', 'The Last Wren Boy', 'Making Friends', 'Till you Hear the Cuckoo Call' and 'When I Pray'.

Revival: 'When I Die'.

Southword: 'The Busker'.

The Cork Literary Review: 'In Memoriam John Moriarty'.

The Doghouse Book of Ballad Poems: 'Help me Make it through the Night'.

The Music of Words (RTE Radio 1): 'The Fiddle Master'.

The Quiet Quarter (Lyric fm): 'A Community Mourns…'.

The SHOp: 'No Blind Eye', 'The Mob Have Surrounded the House, Mammy', 'I'm Glad I Didn't Meet with you, my Boy' and '"Would You Believe"'.

The Stony Thursday Book: 'My Father Hired with Farmers at Fourteen' and 'A Community Mourns…'.

An earlier version of 'My Mother's Burial' was published in *The Flowering Tree/An Crann Faoi Bhláth: Contemporary Irish Poetry with Verse Translations* (Wolfhound Press, Dublin 1991). Acknowledgements are due to Cló Iar Chonnachta for permission to publish this new translation.

Thanks are due to Moira Sweeney for permission to publish my translations from the Irish of Michael Davitt.

And a big thanks to Kris Kristofferson for permission to use lines from his song 'Closer to the Bone' (Jody Ray Publishing) as epigraph to this collection.

Contents

No Blind Eye	19
Ruckard Drury	20
My Father Hired with Farmers at Fourteen	21
A Product to Sell	22
The Traveller Woman	23
The Fiddle Master: Homage to Pádraig O'Keeffe	24
The Busker	25
To My Son As He Leaves Home	26
To My Daughter, Pregnant	27
A Happy Marriage	28
My Mother's Burial	29
The Mob Have Surrounded the House, Mammy	31
I'm Glad I Didn't Meet With You, My Boy	34
Death of a Playwright	35
Death of a Poet	36
In Memoriam John Moriarty	37
The Last Wren Boy	39
Making Friends	40
"Help Me Make It Through The Night"	41
Till You Hear the Cuckoo Call	42
"Would You Believe"	44
A Community Mourns…	45
When I Pray	46
When I Die	47
About the Author	51

Open to the pleasure
Equal to the pain

KRIS KRISTOFFERSON
'Closer to the Bone'

No Blind Eye

For fifty years I've lived in my own place,
There's nothing I don't know about my home,
I admit the ugly but set my face
Towards what I can redeem in song and poem.
For fifty years I've lived in my own place,
In love I tell the truth, turn no blind eye,
I know my people in their sin and grace,
In art I raise them up, do not destroy.
For fifty years I've lived in my own place
While others who don't know the rural scene
Write poems and plays to show only the base:
When art distorts the truth, it is obscene.
For fifty years I've lived in my own place.
What others would distort, I will embrace.

Ruckard Drury

Ruckard Drury, spailpín,
Laboured all his life
For pig-ignorant farmers.
One day, a farmer's wife

Had Drury at her table,
Her fare was tea and bread
But she served him up bad butter
Which Ruckard Drury fed

To a farm-cat at the table
And when the wife saw that,
She turned on the spailpín
Who replied: "Do you see that cat?

You gave me rotten butter;
You saw what he did, no doubt –
That cat there had to lick his arse
To take the taste from his mouth.

That cat there had to lick his arse
The butter was so bad",
Then Drury left her table
And the daily bread it had.

Drury left her table
Hungry still, but proud;
A spailpín, he's remembered
Hungry but unbowed.

Ruckard Drury.

Ruckard Drury: Ruckard (Michael) Drury was born in the Bog Lane, Knockanure, in the parish of Moyvane in 1864 and died in 1952
Spailpín: a migratory farm labourer

My Father Hired with Farmers at Fourteen

My father hired with farmers at fourteen –
No time for school, there were siblings to be fed;
He worked, a servant boy who farmers deemed
Barely worth their shillings and a bed.
My father hired with farmers at fourteen;
He took the boat for England when he could,
A servant boy no more, he'd not be seen
The victim of some farmer's whims and moods.
My father hired with farmers at fourteen
While I, precocious, a selfish little brat
Strutted out book learning. I was mean:
I'd never know the places Dad was at.
My father hired with farmers at fourteen;
He made damn sure his son was free to dream.
Thanks Dad.

A Product to Sell

A product! A product!
A product here to sell!
We'll market it through children
For we know very well
That children get their parents
To indulge them and to buy
Anything from junk food
To the latest useless toy.

A product! A product!
We'll market it through schools,
We'll send 'em gaudy posters
So the kids will think we're cool;
We'll run a competition,
We'll tell 'em what to do –
Collect ten thousand tokens
And we'll give out a few
Computers, televisions,
We'll put 'em into schools
(There's no better advertising
And it's within the rules);
We'll get the schools to enter,
We'll hit the kids and they
Will deliver us their parents.
It's simple. It's child's play.

A product! A product!
A product here to sell!
We'll market it through children…

Salesman, go to hell.

The Traveller Woman

She came out of my childhood
Begging at my door;
The children hadn't seen
A traveller beg before.

She said that God would bless me
For any alms I'd give;
I know the times would tell her
She's got enough to live;

I know the times would tell her
That begging is a crime
But she came into my classroom
From another time.

She came into my classroom
With a basket that would show
The truth of all who looked in it –
We're either yes or no.

She came into my classroom
And I gave. Oh happy day!
She called God's blessings on me
And went upon her way.

The Fiddle Master:
Homage to Pádraig O'Keeffe

For Eugene O'Connell

School's no place for artists who can't take
The ravages of teaching: it destroys
The soul, once full of singing, that must break
As the vision that sustained it shatters, dies.
Not so O'Keeffe, the fiddler: to survive,
He packed the whole thing in one fateful day,
The inspectors on his case, he couldn't thrive
In the classroom. So he left. O'Keeffe would play.
He played throughout Sliabh Luachra where he taught
Music to his people who revere
A musician and a teacher who only sought,
In return for his fiddling, his fill of beer.
It killed him in the end, this way of life,
The man who took a fiddle for his wife.

The Busker

He stood at Brosnan's Corner
With a battered old guitar;
He was drunk – I'd seen him
Stagger from the bar;

His hair was long and matted,
His beard was dirty, black,
His wellies worn and battered,
Over all a tattered mack

Tied with rope around his waist;
He didn't know one song –
His only air was out of tune,
The words were tortured, wrong.

He stood at Brosnan's Corner,
Cinctured by a rope
Singing through creation
His single note of hope.

People passed the corner
In a hurry; none would stop
But some would toss when passing
A coin into his cap.

An hour I watched him singing
With his battered old guitar
Then he took his cap and counted,
And shambled to the bar.

To My Son As He Leaves Home

Son, just to have you 'round the house is good,
The way you make your presence felt. I'll miss
The way that being with you was drink and food;
The future beckons, now it's come to this.
You're leaving, son, I wish you all the best,
May every good that life can give be yours,
Stand firm, love, when life becomes a test,
Remember that the good you do endures.
You're leaving, son, take all you need from me,
It's freely given as it was when you
Needed me, a baby on my knee,
Needed me as to a man you grew.
I love you son, I shed a happy tear
As I let you go in faith and hope and fear.

To My Daughter, Pregnant

She brings me eggs from chickens she has reared,
Cabbages and carrots she has grown,
All the things about her for which I feared
Have come to naught: she's come into her own.
She brings me eggs from chickens she has reared,
Soon she'll be a mother. I rejoice.
Daughter, from the moment you appeared,
You gave me songs to sing in joyful voice.
Soon you'll be a mother and you'll give
Not eggs just but a grandchild to adore,
Another reason for a man to live
For a grandchild adds its blessings to our store.
Pregnant with the life in which you bloom,
You bless us with the child within your womb.

A Happy Marriage

The match was made and on the day,
Because they'd never met,
When the groom and groomsman came to church
She asked "Which one of ye is it?"

She soon found out and in that church
She vowed to live her life
For richer, for poorer, for better, for worse,
A humble country wife.

She cooked for him, she washed, she sewed,
He worked the farm outside –
Were they happy? you might ask;
Well, on the night he died

She told her story to her son,
How his father was a man
He could be rightly proud of;
She let him understand

That all their years of marriage
They lived in unity,
They worked together, prayed together
And did agree.

"When I think of other men", she said,
"He was a cut above;
We were very happy, son,
I've no regrets worth thinking of

But I wonder how it might have been
If we had been in love.
I wonder how it might have been
If we had been in love".

My Mother's Burial

June sun in the orchard
And a silken rustling in the fading day,
An infernal bee humming
Like a screamtearing of the evening's veil.

I was reading an old, soiled letter,
And every word-drink I imbibed
Thorned my heart with bitter pain;
At every single word I read, I cried.

I remembered then the hand that wrote the letter,
A hand recognisable as a face,
A hand that bestowed the mildness of an old Bible,
A hand that was like balsam to my pain.

And then the June fell over into winter
And the orchard became a white cemetery by a stream,
And amid the silent whiteness all around me
Through the snow I could hear the black hole scream.

The brightness of a girl on the day of her First Communion,
The brightness of the host on Sunday on the altar of God,
The brightness of milk flowing freely from the breasts,
When they buried my mother, the brightness of the sod.

While my mind was scourging itself with trying
To taste my mother's burial, whole, complete,
Through the white silence flew so gently
A robin, unflustered, without fear.

She remained above the grave as if knowing
That the reason for her coming was concealed
To all but the one lying waiting in the coffin
And I was jealous of this strange intimacy.

The air of Heaven descended on that grave there,
There was a terrible, holy mirth about that robin,
I was cut off from the mystery like a layman,
The grave was far away though I was beside the coffin.

My lustful soul was cleansed with sweetest sorrow,
On my heart there fell a snow of purity,
In the heart that was made upright I will bury
The memory of her who carried me for three seasons.

The strong men began with their rude shovels
And roughly swept the earth into her grave;
I looked the other way, a neighbour was brushing his knees clean,
I looked at the priest and saw worldliness in his face.

June sun in the orchard
And a silken rustling in the fading day,
An infernal bee humming
Like a screamtearing of the evening's veil.

I am writing small, uneven verses,
I would like to catch a robin's tail,
I would like to banish the knee-brushing spirit,
To journey sadly to the end of day.

From the Irish of Seán Ó Ríordáin (1917-1977)

The Mob Have Surrounded the House, Mammy

The mob have surrounded the house, Mammy,
The mob have surrounded our place,
The mob have surrounded the house, Mammy,
The mob have surrounded our place.
They're wearing white habits, Mammy, gloves and a mask on each face.

They've The Daily Scoop in their hands, Mammy,
Cans of petrol and sharp, sharp knives
They've The Daily Scoop in their hands, Mammy,
Cans of petrol and sharp, sharp knives.
They don't know what for, Mammy, but we'll pay for it with our lives.

They burned a mosque to the ground last night, Mammy,
A library and two churches hereabouts,
They burned a mosque to the ground last night, Mammy,
A library and two churches hereabouts.
They stabbed a tinker woman and cut the tongue from her mouth.

The mob have surrounded the house, Mammy,
The mob have surrounded our place,
The mob have surrounded the house, Mammy,
The mob have surrounded our place.
They're wearing white habits, Mammy, gloves and a mask on each face.

The mob are burning the house, Mammy,
The mob are burning our place,
The mob are burning the house, Mammy,
The mob are burning our place.
They can burn the whole world down, Mammy, but they can't
    burn their hearts' grimace.

From the Irish of Michael Davitt (1950-2005)

I'm Glad I Didn't Meet With You, My Boy

I'm glad I didn't meet with you, my boy,
I'm glad you didn't make it over this way,
I'm glad I don't have to accept this trophy,
I'm glad that I've got to go away.

I'm glad that I'm not glad at the minute,
I'm glad to admit this little bit,
I'm glad, do you understand me?, if I say
That I don't have to be glad every shaggin' day.

From the Irish of Michael Davitt (1950-2005)

Death of a Playwright

In memoriam John B. Keane

"John B. is dead", Listowel said
Incomprehension on its brow;
"John B. is dead", Listowel said,
"We're only an ordinary town now".

Death of a Poet

I stood up for my people,
Out of them I made
A silk purse of a sow's ear.
For this, I was betrayed.

A silk purse of a sow's ear,
For in them I could see
Not Ó Bruadair's total boors
But the stuff of poetry.

A silk purse of a sow's ear,
For this I was betrayed
By gobshites who care nothing
For the beauty I have said.

A silk purse of a sow's ear,
I bid you all good day;
As you leave me, so I leave you.
There is no more to say.

In Memoriam John Moriarty

1.

The chemo did its worst to you
And when your head was bare
A bird flew down from Mangerton
And made a nest out of your hair,
Dear John.

Made a nest of a poet's hair.

2.

You sitting on my mother's bed
Talking literature,
My mother blind, an invalid,
And I am barely four

Listening here in wonder
To words above my head,
All I am begins here
At my mother's bed.

Keats' "Ode to Autumn"
That I misheard as "road",
My mother smiling when I asked:
These conversations sowed

The seeds of all I am today,
The words I learned from you
Who risked your mind, your heart, your soul
That you might live the true.

And it wasn't always beautiful;
In your dark nights you prayed
Your cup would pass even to death –
That was the price you paid

For entering the Labyrinth,
For opening up a road,
A way out for Man and Minotaur.
John, accept this ode

From one who grew from childhood
Picking up your thread,
It is equal to the Minotaur
Theseus left for dead.

The Last Wren Boy

In memoriam Eddie Cunningham

They brought their celebration
To the darkest time of year
Lighting up midwinter
With music, song and beer.

Before Saturn was forgotten,
The Wren Boys played their part;
Now the state we live in
Has breathalysed the heart.

Farewell to winter revelry,
The sacrament of night,
We have no need of Wren Boys
In artificial light.

We have no need of Wren Boys,
We have no need to give
Libation to the darkness
That the light might live.

Farewell to you, last Wren Boy,
You blessed my home today,
You played and drank my whiskey
And went upon your way.

Farewell to you, last Wren Boy,
High Priest of the dark,
You brought your light here with you,
Behind you, left this spark.

You brought your light here with you
And left it in my heart.

Making Friends

For Ola Alexandra Woitusik

She didn't know much English
Nor I much Polish, but
We both loved dogs and rubbed them
Forehead, nose and throat;

She didn't know much English
But we both drew pictures and
Coloured them with crayons –
The language of the hand;

She didn't know much English
But when she sat upon my chair
She patted it with her little hand
That said, "You can sit here";

We couldn't speak in words today
But we could understand
As we made friends all morning
In the new Ireland.

"Help Me Make It Through The Night"

The old lady greets Kristofferson with
"You must listen to my story,
How you helped me make it through the night.

I was a married woman with four children
And my Church decreed it wasn't right
To use contraceptives with my husband
So I'd scrub the floors at bedtime
Till my husband was asleep
And the only company I had,
The only help in my plight,
Was you singing over and over
'Help Me Make it through the Night'.

And how once I was in Saint Patrick's Purgatory,
A penitential island where I went
To walk barefoot, hungry, thirsty
That I might learn what my life meant
And in confession to the priest there
I opened, heart and soul,
And told him that we had four children,
That at nights I scrubbed the floors
Because the Church didn't allow contraceptives,
That, on my knees till my husband slept,
That only then would I cease scrubbing
And retire to our marriage bed.
I asked him to advise me
But he left me dead –
He couldn't help me and my husband
Was all he said.

So know when you sing that song again, Kris,
That I see it in this light –
A woman on her knees scrubbing.

You helped me make it through the night".

Till You Hear the Cuckoo Call

For Fr. Brendan O'Callaghan

Two youngsters on their hillside.
They grew up strong and tall,
Together fished the river,
Together played football.

At eighteen years, the parting –
The one to tend his beasts,
His neighbour to the seminary
To be a priest.

For sixty years, unbroken,
The farmer held his ground,
Married, raised a family,
In mind and body sound;

And then, his old bones aching
From years of toil and chill,
One winter his wife persuades him
To come in from the hill,

That his sons could mind the farm
While he stayed in from the blast
But it played upon his conscience
That he was missing Mass.

Come Lent and in the local church
A Penance Service, though
He still calls it "Confession"
As he learned years ago.

He's driven to "Confession"
Where, to his surprise,
His old neighbour's on the altar
With the other priests this night.

Old friendship not forgotten,
He goes to Father Mick
Who greets him like a brother
And asks him how he is.

The farmer makes confession
Laying bare his life,
Telling his confessor
That, out of love, his wife

Has kept him in this winter,
That he's been missing Mass,
That it bothers him each Sunday
Now the cows are out in grass.

Father Mick is listening
To his neighbour baring all,
"Let you not be in any hurry", he says,
"Till you hear the cuckoo call";

For the priest was once a farmer
And worked this windswept hill
And, absolving his old neighbour,
Brings him from the chill,

The chill that is his conscience,
That doesn't understand
That a time comes when a farmer
Must come in from his land.

And, absolved of his great burden,
He stands up strong and tall
Singing, "I need be in no hurry
Till I hear the cuckoo call".

"I need be in no hurry
Till I hear the cuckoo call".

"Would You Believe"

For Mark Patrick Hederman

"Would You Believe" on TV Sunday night,
"The Church in Crisis" the subject of debate;
I watch it in the pub, my Church's plight,
"The Pope's a Nazi" one drinker snorts in hate.
Everyone here is Catholic; some object
That they come to the pub for company and chat,
Or else a show with which they can connect,
They don't approve what this poor pilgrim's at.
I go to the loo, the channel's changed
To football – religion's turned them off,
(The new religion's sport, I don't complain
As I struggle with my Church let who will scoff),
Catholics ignoring this debate:
The future of their Church. Too late. Too late.

A Community Mourns the Death, by a Freak Accident, of an Eighteen Year Old Boy

We've nothing to fall back on now but prayer
To a God Who's either absent or is dead,
To commend our troubles to His care
Not knowing if He's hearing what is said.
We've nothing to fall back on now but prayer,
To open to the power, the help of words
That they, perhaps, might heal us in despair
As we look into the face of the absurd.
We've nothing to fall back on now but prayer,
The common bond between us in our grief,
The trouble that we shoulder, that we share,
Crying from the trials of belief.
We've nothing to fall back on now but prayer,
The only hope that's left us in despair.

When I Pray

I talk to myself,
The only person
I can't lie to.

Whether God is listening
Or not,
I don't know
But I talk
As if He were.

I talk,
He doesn't answer.
Not that I expect Him to.

But wisdom comes
Through talking
As if God were listening
Where only truth will do.

When I Die

Don't eulogise me with pious lies.

Tell them
I was a man of pubs,
A man of song,
But there were times
When even singing and drinking
Let me down;

Tell them
That I didn't believe enough
In myself or God,
That I didn't always live
As a good man should;

Tell them that I loved
But not enough,
Tell them that loving me
Was often rough;

Tell them I was selfish,
I was vain
But didn't diminish responsibility
Through pain;

Tell them I was no stranger to the dark
But was lit by stars
When the black dogs barked;

Tell them I was honest,
That I lied,
But remember to tell them also
That I tried.

Don't bury me with platitudes
About Christian death.

Say me like I was
And commit me to the earth.

About the Author

GABRIEL FITZMAURICE was born, in 1952, in the village of Moyvane, Co. Kerry where he still lives. For over thirty years he taught in the local primary school from which he retired as principal in 2007. He is author of more than forty books, including collections of poetry in English and Irish as well as several collections of verse for children. He has translated extensively from the Irish and has edited a number of anthologies of poetry in English and Irish. He has published two volumes of essays and collections of songs and ballads. A cassette of his poems, *The Space Between: New and Selected Poems 1984-1992* is also available. He frequently broadcasts on radio and television on education and the arts.

Photograph: Brendan Landy

OTHER BOOKS BY GABRIEL FITZMAURICE

POETRY IN ENGLISH
Rainsong (Beaver Row Press, Dublin, 1984)
Road to the Horizon (Beaver Row Press, 1987)
Dancing Through (Beaver Row Press, 1990)
The Father's Part (Story Line Press, Oregon, 1992)
The Space Between: New and Selected Poems 1984-1992 (Cló Iar-Chonnachta, Conamara, 1993)
The Village Sings (Story Line Press; Cló Iar-Chonnachta; Peterloo Poets, Cornwall, 1996)
A Wrenboy's Carnival: Poems 1980-2000 (Wolfhound Press, Dublin, Peterloo Poets, 2000)
I and the Village (Marino Books, Dublin, 2002)
The Boghole Boys (Marino Books, Cork, 2005)
Twenty One Sonnets (Salmon Poetry, Cliffs of Moher, 2007)
The Essential Gabriel Fitzmaurice (Mercier Press, Cork, 2008)
In Praise of Football (Mercier Press, 2009)

POETRY IN IRISH
Nocht (Coiscéim, Dublin, 1989)
Ag Síobshiúl Chun An Rince (Coiscéim, 1995)
Giolla na nAmhrán: Dánta 1988-1998 (Coiscéim, 1998)

CHILDREN'S POETRY IN ENGLISH
The Moving Stair (The Kerryman, Tralee, 1989)
The Moving Stair (enlarged edition – Poolbeg Press, Dublin, 1993)
But Dad! (Poolbeg Press, 1995)
Puppy and the Sausage (Poolbeg Press, 1998)
Dear Grandad (Poolbeg Press, 2001)
A Giant Never Dies (Poolbeg Press, 2002)
The Oopsy Kid (Poolbeg Press, 2003)
Don't Squash Fluffy (Poolbeg Press, 2004)
I'm Proud to be Me (Mercier Press, 2005)
Really Rotten Rhymes (Mercier Press, 2007)
GF Woz Ere (Mercier Press, 2009)

CHILDREN'S POETRY IN IRISH
Nach Iontach Mar Atá (Cló Iar-Chonnachta, 1994)

CHILDREN'S POETRY IN ENGLISH AND IRISH
Do Teachers Go to the Toilet? / An dTéann Múinteoirí go Tigh an Asail?
(Mercier Press, 2010)

ESSAYS
Kerry on My Mind (Salmon Publishing, 1999)
Beat the Goatskin Till the Goat Cries (Mercier Press, 2006)

TRANSLATION
The Purge (A translation of *An Phurgóid* by Mícheál Ó hAirtnéide) (Beaver Row Press, 1989)
Poems I Wish I'd Written: Translations from the Irish (Cló Iar-Chonnachta, 1996)
The Rhino's Specs / Spéaclaí an tSrónbheannaigh: Selected Children's Poems of Gabriel Rosenstock (Mercier Press, 2002)
Poems from the Irish: Collected Translations (Marino Books, 2004)
Ventry Calling (Mercier Press, 2005)
House, Don't Fall on me (Mercier Press, 2007)

EDITOR
The Flowering Tree / An Crann Faoi Bhláth (contemporary poetry in Irish with verse translations) with Declan Kiberd (Wolfhound Press, 1991)
Between the Hills and Sea: Songs and Ballads of Kerry (Oidhreacht, Ballyheigue, 1991)
Con Greaney: Traditional Singer (Oidhreacht, 1991)
Homecoming / An Bealach 'na Bhaile: Selected Poems of Cathal Ó Searcaigh (Cló Iar-Chonnachta, 1993)
Irish Poetry Now: Other Voices (Wolfhound Press, 1993)
Kerry Through Its Writers (New Island Books, Dublin, 1993)
The Listowel Literary Phenomenon: North Kerry Writers – A Critical Introduction (Cló Iar-Chonnachta, 1994)
Rusty Nails and Astronauts: A Wolfhound Poetry Anthology (Wolfhound Press, 1999) with Robert Dunbar
'The Boro' and 'The Cross': The Parish of Moyvane-Knockanure (The Moyvane-Knockanure Millennium Book Committee, 2000) with Áine Cronin and John Looney
The Kerry Anthology (Marino Books, 2000)
'Come All Good Men and True': Essays from the John B. Keane Symposium (Mercier Press, 2004)
The World of Bryan MacMahon (Mercier Press, 2005)